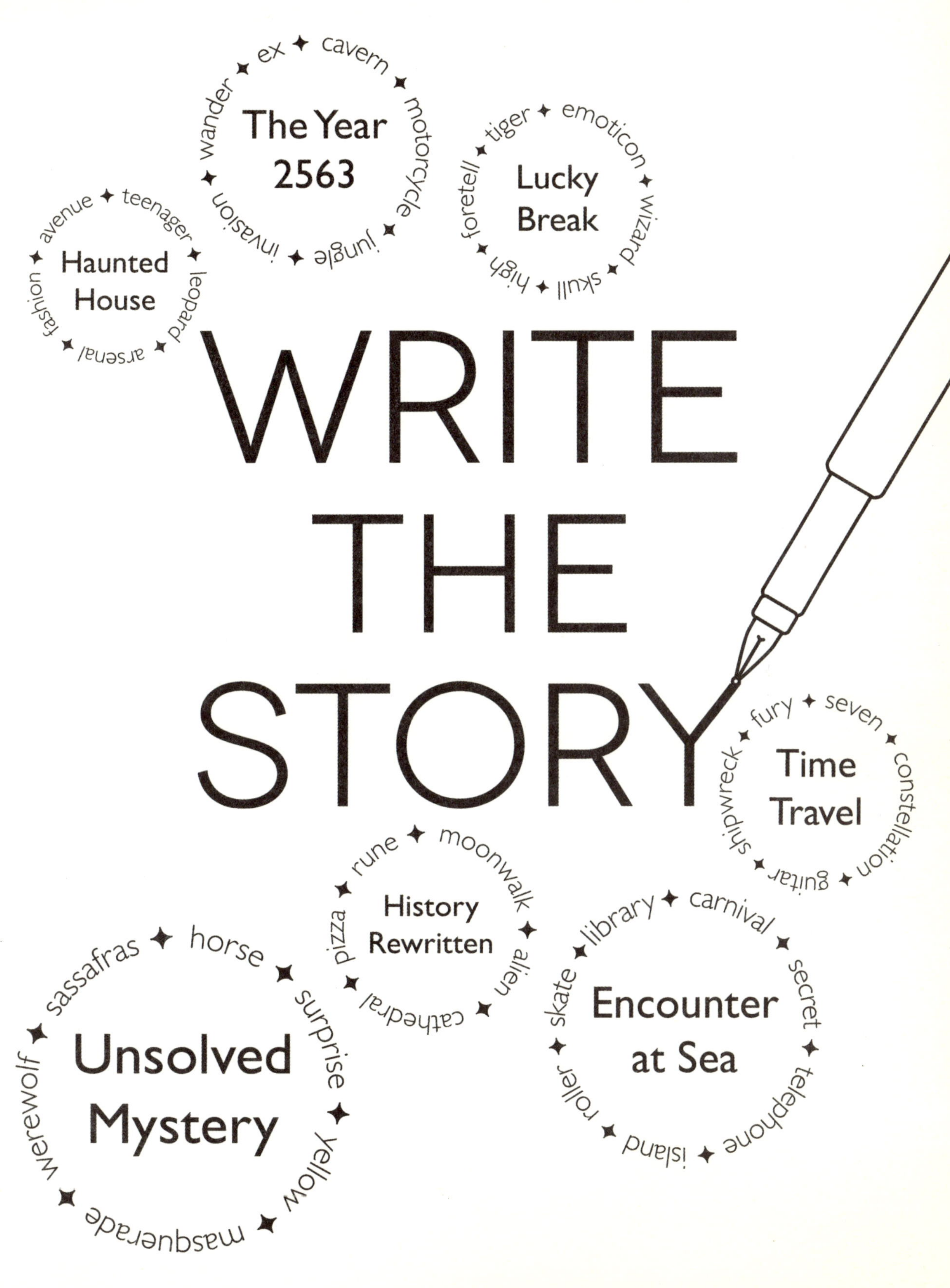
The Year 2563
ex ✦ cavern ✦ motorcycle ✦ jungle ✦ invasion ✦ wander ✦
Lucky Break
tiger ✦ emoticon ✦ wizard ✦ skull ✦ high ✦ foretell ✦
Haunted House
avenue ✦ teenager ✦ leopard ✦ arsenal ✦ fashion ✦
WRITE
THE
STORY
Time Travel
fury ✦ seven ✦ constellation ✦ guitar ✦ shipwreck ✦
History Rewritten
rune ✦ moonwalk ✦ alien ✦ cathedral ✦ pizza ✦
Encounter at Sea
library ✦ carnival ✦ secret ✦ telephone ✦ island ✦ roller ✦ skate ✦
Unsolved Mystery
sassafras ✦ horse ✦ surprise ✦ yellow ✦ masquerade ✦ werewolf ✦

Follow us on social media!

Tag us and use #piccadillyinc in your posts
for a chance to win monthly prizes!

This edition published by Piccadilly (USA) Inc.

Piccadilly (USA) Inc.
12702 Via Cortina, Suite 203
Del Mar, CA 92014
USA

10 9 8 7 6 5 4 3 2 1

Printed in China

ISBN-13: 978-1-60863-453-8

Write the Story: **A Strange Request at a Piano Bar**

Include the following in your story:

✧ *carnival* ✧ *sprained* ✧ *mask* ✧ *oxidation* ✧ *awkward*
✧ *apple* ✧ *juvenile* ✧ *controversy* ✧ *twirl* ✧ *sassafras*

Write the Story: **A Family Mystery Uncovered**

Include the following in your story:

✧ *Sunday* ✧ *secret* ✧ *wallpaper* ✧ *swap* ✧ *sister*
✧ *curiosity* ✧ *island* ✧ *notebook* ✧ *marathon* ✧ *demand*

Write the Story: **Drama In and Out Of the Lab**

Include the following in your story:

✧ *microbiologist* ✧ *telephone* ✧ *hidden* ✧ *bystander* ✧ *trench*
✧ *inside* ✧ *international* ✧ *shoe* ✧ *heights* ✧ *persuade*

Write the Story: **Chasing the Enemy**

Include the following in your story:

✧ *demon* ✧ *bystander* ✧ *escaped* ✧ *parakeet* ✧ *destiny*
✧ *hammer* ✧ *singing* ✧ *ash* ✧ *cathedral* ✧ *heels*

Write the Story: **An Unexpected Union**

Include the following in your story:

✧ *brothers* ✧ *potato* ✧ *common* ✧ *hands* ✧ *boyfriend*
✧ *alphabet* ✧ *scribble* ✧ *hydrangea* ✧ *sandwich* ✧ *tug-of-war*

Write the Story: **A Lunch Date Gone Wrong**

Include the following in your story:

- *eruption*
- *salad*
- *fire*
- *career*
- *assume*
- *roller skate*
- *draw*
- *promise*
- *full moon*
- *sweet*

Write the Story: **Business as UNusual**

Include the following in your story:

✧ *housewife* ✧ *moonwalk* ✧ *dog* ✧ *basement* ✧ *conclude*
✧ *alien* ✧ *ignore* ✧ *lightning* ✧ *embrace* ✧ *time*

Write the Story: **The Year Is 2563 ...**

Include the following in your story:

✧ *space station* ✧ *knuckle* ✧ *interview* ✧ *horse* ✧ *twenty-seven*
✧ *lipstick* ✧ *transformation* ✧ *studio* ✧ *distribution* ✧ *assert*

Write the Story: **Friends on the Town**

Include the following in your story:

✧ *pizza* ✧ *booth* ✧ *college* ✧ *restore* ✧ *collection*
✧ *rip* ✧ *Buffalo wings* ✧ *chiffon* ✧ *butcher* ✧ *display*

Write the Story: **Today at the Amusement Park**

Include the following in your story:

✧ *Ferris wheel* ✧ *revive* ✧ *dinosaur* ✧ *split* ✧ *disk*
✧ *assumption* ✧ *exceed* ✧ *narrow* ✧ *snickerdoodle* ✧ *join*

Write the Story: **A Day in the Life**

Include the following in your story:

✧ *identical* ✧ *pot roast* ✧ *decorate* ✧ *sign* ✧ *abuse*
✧ *library* ✧ *amnesia* ✧ *butcher* ✧ *submit* ✧ *sensation*

Write the Story: **The Last Moment of Childhood**

Include the following in your story:

✧ *Halloween* ✧ *refrigerator* ✧ *pier* ✧ *strengthen* ✧ *voices*
✧ *surprise* ✧ *contribute* ✧ *bird* ✧ *iron* ✧ *requirement*

Write the Story: **Wrapping Up a Business Trip**

Include the following in your story:

✧ *bar* ✧ *laptop* ✧ *insect* ✧ *Germany* ✧ *baseball*
✧ *nervous* ✧ *embark* ✧ *protest* ✧ *swing* ✧ *sentence*

Write the Story: **A Couple on a Cruise**

Include the following in your story:

✧ *nosy* ✧ *sponsor* ✧ *passenger* ✧ *willing* ✧ *smile*
✧ *brew* ✧ *yellow* ✧ *neighbor* ✧ *hundred* ✧ *stairwell*

Write the Story: **Unsolved Mystery**

Include the following in your story:

✧ *murder* ✧ *green* ✧ *agreement* ✧ *traditional* ✧ *carpenter*
✧ *snake* ✧ *sugar* ✧ *kidney* ✧ *congress* ✧ *jam*

Write the Story: **Magic Interferes in New Orleans**

Include the following in your story:

✧ *matriarch* ✧ *throat* ✧ *impossible* ✧ *vinegar* ✧ *apology*
✧ *slice* ✧ *microwave* ✧ *raspberry* ✧ *choose* ✧ *snore*

Write the Story: **A Romantic Scene in an Unromantic Place**

Include the following in your story:

✧ *blacksmith* ✧ *tongue* ✧ *woman* ✧ *spark* ✧ *musical*
✧ *blind* ✧ *Bible* ✧ *barbeque* ✧ *elbow* ✧ *bundle*

Write the Story: **On a Quest**

Include the following in your story:

✧ *medieval* ✧ *derive* ✧ *molten* ✧ *oar* ✧ *rhythm*
✧ *ears* ✧ *antique* ✧ *corn* ✧ *daughter* ✧ *yammer*

Write the Story: **The Supernatural Invades the Everyday**

Include the following in your story:

✧ *metamorphosis* ✧ *rogue* ✧ *shrug* ✧ *salamander* ✧ *sleepy*
✧ *chimpanzee* ✧ *enzyme* ✧ *lemon* ✧ *glance* ✧ *merge*

Write the Story: **A Journalist Crosses the Line**

Include the following in your story:

✧ *defamation* ✧ *stroke* ✧ *reporter* ✧ *truck* ✧ *weasel*
✧ *supermarket* ✧ *encyclopedia* ✧ *contemplate* ✧ *classify* ✧ *clutch*

Write the Story: **Big Time Deals in the Big City**

Include the following in your story:

✧ *feud* ✧ *philosophy* ✧ *palace* ✧ *finger* ✧ *scandal*
✧ *skyscraper* ✧ *complacent* ✧ *handle* ✧ *crawl* ✧ *challenge*

Write the Story: **A Scientist Makes an Unexpected Discovery**

Include the following in your story:

✧ *parallel* ✧ *informal* ✧ *crude* ✧ *expand* ✧ *popular*
✧ *unlikely* ✧ *analyst* ✧ *replacement* ✧ *cell* ✧ *chest*

Write the Story: **Students Take on a Challenge**

Include the following in your story:

✧ *masquerade* ✧ *gang* ✧ *allege* ✧ *double* ✧ *lucky*
✧ *tea* ✧ *personality* ✧ *introduction* ✧ *parasite* ✧ *class*

Write the Story: **Office Intrigue in the Future**

Include the following in your story:

✧ *time travel* ✧ *trousers* ✧ *supervise* ✧ *successfully* ✧ *law*
✧ *identity* ✧ *mustard* ✧ *kitchen* ✧ *tooth* ✧ *fly*

Write the Story: **Political Machinations**

Include the following in your story:

✧ *appointment* ✧ *dangerous* ✧ *cost* ✧ *empire* ✧ *kitten*
✧ *mug* ✧ *converter* ✧ *essence* ✧ *tennis* ✧ *poke*

Write the Story: **History Rewritten**

Include the following in your story:

✧ *funeral* ✧ *condemn* ✧ *distribution* ✧ *button* ✧ *sink*
✧ *art* ✧ *jealousy* ✧ *brain* ✧ *tax* ✧ *lover*

Write the Story: **On the Campaign Trail**

Include the following in your story:

✧ *president*	✧ *dove*	✧ *tremble*	✧ *column*	✧ *united*
✧ *secretary*	✧ *impression*	✧ *soup*	✧ *milk*	✧ *armor*

Write the Story: **The Problems of Celebrities**

Include the following in your story:

✧ *tabloid* ✧ *existence* ✧ *dolphin* ✧ *bunker* ✧ *surgery*
✧ *parade* ✧ *chase* ✧ *master* ✧ *smash* ✧ *possum*

Write the Story: **Tension in Suburbia**

Include the following in your story:

✧ *muffled* ✧ *medical* ✧ *orchid* ✧ *par* ✧ *reign*
✧ *animal* ✧ *church* ✧ *shirt* ✧ *snatch* ✧ *grin*

Write the Story: **The Gala Event of the Season**

Include the following in your story:

✧ *cater waiter* ✧ *suspicious* ✧ *architecture* ✧ *money* ✧ *switch*
✧ *imagine* ✧ *yawn* ✧ *blot* ✧ *lilac* ✧ *program*

Write the Story: **The Love of Each Other's Lives**

Include the following in your story:

✧ *piano* ✧ *fish* ✧ *store* ✧ *ceiling fan* ✧ *behave*
✧ *breathe* ✧ *describe* ✧ *irritating* ✧ *enthusiastically* ✧ *righteous*

Write the Story: **A Much Needed Vacation**

Include the following in your story:

✧ *hair salon* ✧ *burn* ✧ *escape* ✧ *waste* ✧ *yesterday*
✧ *quack* ✧ *quaint* ✧ *jittery* ✧ *bob* ✧ *expensive*

Write the Story: **First Love**

Include the following in your story:

✧ *dog walker* ✧ *observe* ✧ *frightful* ✧ *broken* ✧ *curvy*
✧ *wooden* ✧ *violet* ✧ *rabbit* ✧ *stamp* ✧ *maze*

Write the Story: **Circus Performers are People, Too**

Include the following in your story:

- ✧ *confrontation*
- ✧ *clap*
- ✧ *coach*
- ✧ *zoom*
- ✧ *tumbler*
- ✧ *clumsy*
- ✧ *digestion*
- ✧ *letter*
- ✧ *giant*
- ✧ *whip*

Write the Story: **A Bartender's Best Night Ever**

Include the following in your story:

✧ *airport* ✧ *appreciate* ✧ *curve* ✧ *grumpy* ✧ *ruthless*
✧ *record* ✧ *nerve* ✧ *acoustics* ✧ *alarm* ✧ *expert*

Write the Story: **A Small, Local Political Race**

Include the following in your story:

✧ *coordinated* ✧ *support* ✧ *farmhand* ✧ *spray* ✧ *serious*
✧ *rail* ✧ *lips* ✧ *taxpayer* ✧ *fool* ✧ *meddler*

Write the Story: **A New Love Blooms in Old Age**

Include the following in your story:

✧ *inheritance* ✧ *walk* ✧ *dust* ✧ *dapper* ✧ *husky*
✧ *squirrel* ✧ *plantation* ✧ *berry* ✧ *silk* ✧ *shovel*

Write the Story: **A Family-Run Farm**

Include the following in your story:

✧ *temporary* ✧ *invent* ✧ *trust* ✧ *horse* ✧ *burst*
✧ *pulley* ✧ *signal* ✧ *dam* ✧ *punch* ✧ *checker*

Write the Story: **A Support Group Meeting**

Include the following in your story:

✧ *novelist* ✧ *fountain* ✧ *snow* ✧ *lady* ✧ *pastoral*
✧ *communicate* ✧ *scene* ✧ *sprout* ✧ *carve* ✧ *whisper*

Write the Story: **Behind The Scenes at the Theater**

Include the following in your story:

✧ *loneliness* ✧ *applaud* ✧ *beg* ✧ *jogging* ✧ *memorize*
✧ *admit* ✧ *solitude* ✧ *converse* ✧ *eternity* ✧ *marsh*

Write the Story: **On Main Street in a Small Town**

Include the following in your story:

- *square*
- *separate*
- *type*
- *truculent*
- *preach*
- *wilderness*
- *pang*
- *façade*
- *pawn*
- *pavement*

Write the Story: **Running Away From Change**

Include the following in your story:

✧ *flight* ✧ *blacktop* ✧ *tense* ✧ *contemplation* ✧ *window*
✧ *enclosure* ✧ *spit* ✧ *blink* ✧ *trade* ✧ *fence*

Write the Story: **A Police Investigation**

Include the following in your story:

✧ *ominous* ✧ *arrest* ✧ *decay* ✧ *squeal* ✧ *reduce*
✧ *feline* ✧ *avoid* ✧ *feet* ✧ *blackberry* ✧ *bark*

Write the Story: **A Woman's First Day in a Convent**

Include the following in your story:

✧ *nun* ✧ *zealous* ✧ *grateful* ✧ *statue* ✧ *lick*
✧ *attend* ✧ *film* ✧ *page* ✧ *recognize* ✧ *pomegranate*

Write the Story: **A Fishing Trip**

Include the following in your story:

✧ *jig* ✧ *unsightly* ✧ *wait* ✧ *beam* ✧ *shoulder*
✧ *grey* ✧ *reminder* ✧ *mouth* ✧ *Canada* ✧ *river*

Write the Story: **Living with a Chronic Illness**

Include the following in your story:

✧ *fever* ✧ *weight* ✧ *unpack* ✧ *rollercoaster* ✧ *surgeon*
✧ *daffodil* ✧ *Northern* ✧ *patch* ✧ *mossy* ✧ *tendril*

Write the Story: **Doctors Off Duty**

Include the following in your story:

✧ *goose* ✧ *anatomy* ✧ *Spanish* ✧ *pitcher* ✧ *topography*
✧ *smoke* ✧ *homeward* ✧ *gritty* ✧ *sailor* ✧ *salt*

Write the Story: **Two Best Friends are Baristas**

Include the following in your story:

✧ *coffee* ✧ *molehill* ✧ *insulation* ✧ *sneakers* ✧ *inspire*
✧ *pencil* ✧ *embroidery* ✧ *justify* ✧ *loveless* ✧ *pane*

Write the Story: **A Middle Class Family Doing Its Best**

Include the following in your story:

✧ *castle* ✧ *beetle* ✧ *Facebook* ✧ *calculator* ✧ *nostril*
✧ *timetable* ✧ *wireless* ✧ *stripes* ✧ *scroll* ✧ *white*

Write the Story: **An Intern Meets Someone for Lunch**

Include the following in your story:

✧ *father* ✧ *continent* ✧ *favorite* ✧ *comfortable* ✧ *highlight*
✧ *drive* ✧ *salesman* ✧ *pair* ✧ *mail* ✧ *level*

Write the Story: **A Babysitter Snoops and Finds Something Unexpected**

Include the following in your story:

✧ *newspaper* ✧ *cardinal* ✧ *cotton* ✧ *document* ✧ *tiramisu*
✧ *blackened* ✧ *prediction* ✧ *borderline* ✧ *freedom* ✧ *female*

Write the Story: **A Fortune Cookie Comes True**

Include the following in your story:

✧ *numerology* ✧ *hilarious* ✧ *dictionary* ✧ *recycled* ✧ *brick*
✧ *ocean* ✧ *meaningful* ✧ *garbage* ✧ *star* ✧ *origin*

Write the Story: **Having the Boss Over For Dinner**

Include the following in your story:

✧ *cerulean* ✧ *chair* ✧ *joyous* ✧ *meatloaf* ✧ *pallid*
✧ *brioche* ✧ *monthly* ✧ *thirteen* ✧ *forehead* ✧ *video*

Write the Story: **A Camping Trip in Which No One Has Ever Been Camping Before**

Include the following in your story:

✧ *constellation* ✧ *ketchup* ✧ *royal* ✧ *gear* ✧ *atmosphere*
✧ *expand* ✧ *livid* ✧ *example* ✧ *luminous* ✧ *moonlit*

Write the Story: **The Night Before Graduation**

Include the following in your story:

✧ *obscene* ✧ *margarita* ✧ *paradise* ✧ *story* ✧ *tempo*
✧ *truthfully* ✧ *stonewall* ✧ *plain* ✧ *opposite* ✧ *loan*

Write the Story: **A Strange Proposition From a Stranger**

Include the following in your story:

✧ *sequin* ✧ *luncheon* ✧ *designer* ✧ *toolbox* ✧ *measurement*
✧ *force* ✧ *dented* ✧ *cellular* ✧ *banish* ✧ *lock*

Write the Story: **A Mysterious Package**

Include the following in your story:

✧ *theater*	✧ *almond*	✧ *version*	✧ *triple*	✧ *arrow*
✧ *pathway*	✧ *man*	✧ *mangle*	✧ *drapery*	✧ *bullet*

Write the Story: **Fired From a Long-Term Job**

Include the following in your story:

✧ *guitar* ✧ *military* ✧ *aversion* ✧ *mouse* ✧ *vertical*
✧ *crumple* ✧ *runaway* ✧ *creation* ✧ *alphabetize* ✧ *tablet*

Write the Story: **A New Take on the Arthurian Legend**

Include the following in your story:

✧ *Avalon* ✧ *crossbow* ✧ *orphan* ✧ *list* ✧ *comrade*

✧ *corruption* ✧ *lake* ✧ *enfold* ✧ *disgraceful* ✧ *grass*

Write the Story: **Anonymous Gifts Start Arriving at the Doorstep**

Include the following in your story:

✧ *teenager* ✧ *camouflage* ✧ *birch* ✧ *harmony* ✧ *rifle*
✧ *screen door* ✧ *wrinkle* ✧ *dive* ✧ *pick-up* ✧ *sticker*

Write the Story: **Mash Up Two Classic Fairy Tales into One Story**

Include the following in your story:

✧ *fireplace* ✧ *sword* ✧ *grove* ✧ *stoke* ✧ *underbrush*
✧ *mourn* ✧ *seven* ✧ *friendship* ✧ *cardboard* ✧ *giver*

Write the Story: **A Missionary in a Remote Village**

Include the following in your story:

✧ *orchestra* ✧ *finch* ✧ *aim* ✧ *development* ✧ *ex*
✧ *bold* ✧ *old-fashioned* ✧ *gut* ✧ *brassy* ✧ *sharp*

Write the Story: **A Teenager Whose Parents Have Unwelcome News**

Include the following in your story:

✧ *comic book* ✧ *battery* ✧ *crumbly* ✧ *apartment* ✧ *angelic*
✧ *breach* ✧ *shooter* ✧ *soda* ✧ *engineer* ✧ *substantiate*

Write the Story: **A Shooting in a Public Place**

Include the following in your story:

✧ *shipwreck* ✧ *pummel* ✧ *nurse* ✧ *structure* ✧ *home*
✧ *offset* ✧ *cabin* ✧ *puppy* ✧ *knot* ✧ *tide*

Write the Story: **Picking Up a Hitchhiker**

Include the following in your story:

✧ *hospital* ✧ *defer* ✧ *interface* ✧ *experiment* ✧ *beaker*
✧ *visualize* ✧ *mattress* ✧ *skyline* ✧ *interpret* ✧ *zap*

Write the Story: **Selling a Childhood Home**

Include the following in your story:

✧ *dreamscape* ✧ *convince* ✧ *pioneer* ✧ *genesis* ✧ *cumulous*
✧ *jump* ✧ *mash* ✧ *condition* ✧ *erase* ✧ *gold*

Write the Story: **A Wild Animal Loose in the House**

Include the following in your story:

✧ *pregnant* ✧ *community* ✧ *logo* ✧ *statistics* ✧ *democracy*
✧ *honesty* ✧ *criminal* ✧ *ankle* ✧ *orange* ✧ *comment*

Write the Story: **A Midlife Career Change**

Include the following in your story:

✧ *chef* ✧ *upgrade* ✧ *monkey* ✧ *turkey* ✧ *fashion*
✧ *team* ✧ *harden* ✧ *noon* ✧ *elevator* ✧ *baste*

Write the Story: **A Ghost Story**

Include the following in your story:

✧ *tango* ✧ *diversify* ✧ *blog* ✧ *invisible* ✧ *missile*
✧ *glitter* ✧ *scuff* ✧ *balloon* ✧ *bird cage* ✧ *grizzly bear*

Write the Story: **The Main Character Thinks He or She is About to Get Fired**

Include the following in your story:

✧ *magazine* ✧ *blow-dryer* ✧ *congeal* ✧ *bluebell* ✧ *cummerbund*
✧ *wheelie bag* ✧ *pastels* ✧ *cheeseburger* ✧ *binding* ✧ *science*

Write the Story: **A Coastal Town in New England is Full of Crazy Characters**

Include the following in your story:

✧ *lobsterman* ✧ *bicycle* ✧ *light bulb* ✧ *yoga* ✧ *fireworks*
✧ *infantile* ✧ *weave* ✧ *leopard* ✧ *balding* ✧ *sunset*

Write the Story: **A Haunted House**

Include the following in your story:

✧ *silver* ✧ *relativity* ✧ *watercolor* ✧ *Copper Beech* ✧ *limited*
✧ *affect* ✧ *broccoli* ✧ *politician* ✧ *arsenal* ✧ *cufflink*

Write the Story: **Something Bad is About to Happen, But Nobody Believes the Main Character**

Include the following in your story:

✧ *Andromeda* ✧ *stop sign* ✧ *dandelion* ✧ *iceberg* ✧ *spectacle*
✧ *poet* ✧ *candle lit* ✧ *keyboard* ✧ *bumble* ✧ *robotic*

Write the Story: **A Writer with Noisy Neighbors**

Include the following in your story:

✧ *dentist* ✧ *rainbow* ✧ *explosion* ✧ *horizon* ✧ *cactus*
✧ *palm* ✧ *Saturday* ✧ *latte* ✧ *beets* ✧ *sample*

Write the Story: **Newlyweds on Their Honeymoon**

Include the following in your story:

✧ *cockpit* ✧ *selfie* ✧ *kayak* ✧ *thought bubble* ✧ *picnic table*
✧ *wander* ✧ *propose* ✧ *shiatsu* ✧ *motherhood* ✧ *temple*

Write the Story: **The Main Character Goes on a Trip Alone to Gain Perspective**

Include the following in your story:

✧ *lighthouse* ✧ *flock* ✧ *muscle* ✧ *sprinkle* ✧ *insult*
✧ *cliffhanger* ✧ *cheetah* ✧ *chartreuse* ✧ *wrist* ✧ *seedling*

Write the Story: **A Character with OCD in the Worst Possible Situation**

Include the following in your story:

✧ *monastery* ✧ *chalkboard* ✧ *elephant* ✧ *coast* ✧ *turmeric*
✧ *poppy* ✧ *defeat* ✧ *chessboard* ✧ *inhumane* ✧ *search*

Write the Story: **An Alien in Disguise Among Humans**

Include the following in your story:

✧ *Aurora Borealis* ✧ *paint brush* ✧ *corn field* ✧ *cluster* ✧ *lineup*
✧ *overlook* ✧ *suspect* ✧ *bridge* ✧ *dome* ✧ *dash*

Write the Story: **A Young Child Makes a Discovery**

Include the following in your story:

✧ *Superman* ✧ *ginkgo biloba* ✧ *cavern* ✧ *clicker* ✧ *aloe*
✧ *moviegoer* ✧ *stretch* ✧ *furry* ✧ *yardstick* ✧ *makeup*

Write the Story: **High School Hierarchy**

Include the following in your story:

✧ *pyramid* ✧ *cowboy hat* ✧ *amateurish* ✧ *angle* ✧ *ripple*
✧ *cheese* ✧ *jersey* ✧ *blister* ✧ *odyssey* ✧ *reorder*

Write the Story: **The Main Character has Amnesia**

Include the following in your story:

✧ *antiquarian* ✧ *satellite* ✧ *cinnamon* ✧ *fortune* ✧ *cookie*
✧ *harbor* ✧ *cedar* ✧ *invitation* ✧ *soccer* ✧ *annual* ✧ *speaker*

Write the Story: **The Early Days of the Zombie Apocalypse**

Include the following in your story:

✧ *motherboard* ✧ *buffalo* ✧ *Eiffel Tower* ✧ *raven* ✧ *motorcycle*
✧ *envelope* ✧ *tulip* ✧ *moon* ✧ *reflect* ✧ *sycamore*

Write the Story: **Adult Friends on Vacation in the Tropics**

Include the following in your story:

✧ *scuba diver* ✧ *champagne* ✧ *invasion* ✧ *archway* ✧ *hoard*
✧ *strawberry* ✧ *penguin* ✧ *autumnal* ✧ *cease* ✧ *mist*

Write the Story: **The Main Character Thwarts Traditional Gender Roles**

Include the following in your story:

✧ *woman* ✧ *bestseller* ✧ *buttress* ✧ *goldfish* ✧ *barnyard*
✧ *walkway* ✧ *crop* ✧ *winter* ✧ *driveway* ✧ *steer*

Write the Story: **Memory Editing Wreaks Havoc**

Include the following in your story:

✧ *Jupiter* ✧ *chocolate* ✧ *domestic* ✧ *blossom* ✧ *ladder*
✧ *steam* ✧ *extension* ✧ *pine cone* ✧ *sunrise* ✧ *tide*

Write the Story: **A Tour Guide in the Florida Keys**

Include the following in your story:

✧ *revolver* ✧ *headphones* ✧ *doughnut* ✧ *leopard* ✧ *spaghetti*

✧ *tiki hut* ✧ *magma* ✧ *magnetize* ✧ *swampy* ✧ *recital*

Write the Story: **A Dystopian Glimpse of the Future**

Include the following in your story:

✧ *wheelchair* ✧ *Labrador* ✧ *throne* ✧ *jungle* ✧ *prescription*
✧ *railroad* ✧ *trunk* ✧ *gulley* ✧ *wasp* ✧ *photosynthesize*

Write the Story: **A Letter Changes Everything**

Include the following in your story:

✧ *alchemist* ✧ *waterfall* ✧ *birthday* ✧ *cottage* ✧ *spring*
✧ *roar* ✧ *syrup* ✧ *sift* ✧ *immeasurable* ✧ *bank*

Write the Story: **Getting Away with Murder**

Include the following in your story:

✧ *Snow Queen* ✧ *windmill* ✧ *tunnel* ✧ *childhood* ✧ *endanger*
✧ *cypress* ✧ *wine* ✧ *horseback* ✧ *temperature* ✧ *imperial*

Write the Story: **A Sales Manager Has Had Enough**

Include the following in your story:

✧ *Australia* ✧ *faith* ✧ *gullet* ✧ *customer* ✧ *butterfly*

✧ *headlight* ✧ *badger* ✧ *shoreline* ✧ *mountain* ✧ *owl*

Write the Story: **Something Believed to Be Myth is Very Real**

Include the following in your story:

✧ *necromancer* ✧ *elm* ✧ *roadmap* ✧ *GPS* ✧ *outside*
✧ *twine* ✧ *water lily* ✧ *plastic* ✧ *chopper* ✧ *powerless*

Write the Story: **Based on a True Story**

Include the following in your story:

✧ *Mongols* ✧ *exception* ✧ *gosling* ✧ *elementary* ✧ *coordinate*
✧ *solution* ✧ *tighten* ✧ *shuffle* ✧ *horseshoe* ✧ *universe*

Write the Story: **Reliving Childhood Memories as an Adult**

Include the following in your story:

- *target practice*
- *bookmark*
- *wizard*
- *determination*
- *unbridled*
- *schedule*
- *forward*
- *pork loin*
- *innermost*
- *supposition*

Write the Story: **A Story Pulled From Today's Headlines and Rewritten**

Include the following in your story:

✧ *boxer* ✧ *cherry blossom* ✧ *magic* ✧ *implement* ✧ *artwork*
✧ *safety* ✧ *chime* ✧ *chain link* ✧ *towel* ✧ *ingredient*

Write the Story: **The Villain is Really the Hero**

Include the following in your story:

✧ *witchcraft* ✧ *recommend* ✧ *sand dollar* ✧ *fisticuff* ✧ *paprika*
✧ *eyeball* ✧ *nightlight* ✧ *gibberish* ✧ *infuriating* ✧ *dreadful*

Write the Story: **The Main Character Has Woken Up Missing One of the Five Senses**

Include the following in your story:

- ✧ *piracy*
- ✧ *parking*
- ✧ *seashell*
- ✧ *selfish*
- ✧ *adjustment*
- ✧ *lax*
- ✧ *slumber*
- ✧ *fragrance*
- ✧ *saltine*
- ✧ *top hat*

Write the Story: **A Story Told Through Emails**

Include the following in your story:

✧ *philanthropist* ✧ *symmetrical* ✧ *terminate* ✧ *noodle* ✧ *emoticon*
✧ *reference* ✧ *sunglasses* ✧ *moonlight* ✧ *borrow* ✧ *newsletter*

Write the Story: **Parents Solve a Problem Together**

Include the following in your story:

✧ *rhinoceros* ✧ *umbrella* ✧ *announcement* ✧ *petal* ✧ *feather*
✧ *fruit* ✧ *placemat* ✧ *sketch* ✧ *wobble* ✧ *boil*

Write the Story: **An Alligator on the Loose**

Include the following in your story:

✧ *New York City* ✧ *Chewbacca* ✧ *typical* ✧ *beard* ✧ *walkabout*
✧ *interrupt* ✧ *clang* ✧ *belly* ✧ *cockatoo* ✧ *stroll*

Write the Story: **Magic in Everyday Occurences**

Include the following in your story:

✧ *Krav Maga* ✧ *touch screen* ✧ *litter* ✧ *vendor* ✧ *doorbell*
✧ *finish* ✧ *hungry* ✧ *aversion* ✧ *signature* ✧ *sweatband*

Write the Story: **A Story That Takes Place in One Room**

Include the following in your story:

✧ *petting zoo* ✧ *handsome* ✧ *unbound* ✧ *annoy* ✧ *weekend*

✧ *invest* ✧ *immortal* ✧ *piglet* ✧ *cocktail* ✧ *camp*

Write the Story: **An Unexpected Visitor Shakes Things Up**

Include the following in your story:

✧ *tightrope* ✧ *nightingale* ✧ *underline* ✧ *risk* ✧ *academy*
✧ *existential* ✧ *outlook* ✧ *Friday* ✧ *gobble* ✧ *grill*

Write the Story: **A Hairdresser Received a Shocking Confession from a Customer**

Include the following in your story:

✧ *poverty* ✧ *marksman* ✧ *bookshelf* ✧ *backspace* ✧ *hedge*
✧ *cuckoo* ✧ *pumpkin* ✧ *courteous* ✧ *deduction* ✧ *acute*

Write the Story: **War on Foreign Soil**

Include the following in your story:

✧ *amputated* ✧ *global* ✧ *curtain* ✧ *banana* ✧ *carbonate*

✧ *calisthenics* ✧ *patriot* ✧ *walnut* ✧ *fixture* ✧ *bluetooth*

Write the Story: **A Conversation Between Artists**

Include the following in your story:

✧ *skull* ✧ *galaxy* ✧ *expression* ✧ *trash can* ✧ *deployment*
✧ *visitor* ✧ *brushstroke* ✧ *decade* ✧ *forgot* ✧ *ponder*

Write the Story: **A Dinner Party**

Include the following in your story:

✧ *phoenix* ✧ *canvas* ✧ *homesick* ✧ *evening* ✧ *spicy*
✧ *rooftop* ✧ *cicada* ✧ *orthodox* ✧ *ding* ✧ *spruce*

Write the Story: **A Night at the Opera**

Include the following in your story:

✧ *Air Force* ✧ *crane* ✧ *orchestrate* ✧ *leotard* ✧ *stubble*
✧ *pinpoint* ✧ *placate* ✧ *machete* ✧ *photo* ✧ *pivot*

Write the Story: **A Suspected Affair**

Include the following in your story:

✧ *marriage* ✧ *checklist* ✧ *songbird* ✧ *mango* ✧ *ranch*
✧ *stroke* ✧ *magpie* ✧ *scowl* ✧ *simper* ✧ *commotion*

Write the Story: **Conspiracy Theorists Convention**

Include the following in your story:

✧ *crop circles* ✧ *vacation* ✧ *possum* ✧ *filibuster* ✧ *mutiny*
✧ *scour* ✧ *compass* ✧ *drift* ✧ *drawback* ✧ *electric*

Write the Story: **The Main Character Witnesses a Crime**

Include the following in your story:

- *Christmas*
- *almond*
- *paisley*
- *lion*
- *pipe*
- *scream*
- *fade*
- *French horn*
- *inflate*
- *maple*

Write the Story: **The Loss of a Loved One**

Include the following in your story:

✧ *bachelor* ✧ *chandelier* ✧ *ladybug* ✧ *Muslim* ✧ *strive*
✧ *inverse* ✧ *mannerism* ✧ *balance* ✧ *overreact* ✧ *prime*

Write the Story: **A Lucky Break**

Include the following in your story:

✧ *City Hall* ✧ *feminist* ✧ *myth* ✧ *interpreter* ✧ *maverick*
✧ *raccoon* ✧ *radiant* ✧ *scram* ✧ *off switch* ✧ *logic*

Write the Story: **Tumultuous Soulmates are on Opposing Sides of a Conflict**

Include the following in your story:

✧ *apothecary* ✧ *bow tie* ✧ *ladylike* ✧ *sprocket* ✧ *mushroom*
✧ *scrounge* ✧ *frenzy* ✧ *match* ✧ *oust* ✧ *prisoner*

Write the Story: **An Interrupted Journey**

Include the following in your story:

✧ *butterfly effect* ✧ *vulture* ✧ *cramp* ✧ *industry* ✧ *purge*
✧ *scruple* ✧ *snorkel* ✧ *snitch* ✧ *warning* ✧ *unless*

Write the Story: **A Hike Through the Woods**

Include the following in your story:

✧ *leprechaun* ✧ *covert* ✧ *fireball* ✧ *snoop* ✧ *wart*
✧ *pity* ✧ *backpack* ✧ *practice* ✧ *nausea* ✧ *collar*

Write the Story: **The Best Night the Main Character Won't Remember**

Include the following in your story:

- *Mardi Gras*
- *puzzle*
- *scorpion*
- *snout*
- *ward*
- *cooler*
- *shake*
- *tiger*
- *exhausted*
- *stumble*

Write the Story: **An Anthropologist at a Costume Party**

Include the following in your story:

✧ *fashionista* ✧ *responsibility* ✧ *cruelty* ✧ *article* ✧ *arrangement*
✧ *frog* ✧ *french fries* ✧ *calf* ✧ *braid* ✧ *addition*

Write the Story: **A Crime Scene**

Include the following in your story:

✧ *phantom* ✧ *desperate* ✧ *scale* ✧ *normality* ✧ *ponytail*
✧ *tremendous* ✧ *stiletto* ✧ *hound* ✧ *wrinkle* ✧ *smoke*

Write the Story: **A Countdown**

Include the following in your story:

✧ *plumber* ✧ *witty* ✧ *oyster* ✧ *voluntary* ✧ *asparagus*

✧ *centralize* ✧ *judge* ✧ *puddle* ✧ *pointer* ✧ *ampersand*

Write the Story: **A Child's Dream Literally Comes True**

Include the following in your story:

✧ *high school* ✧ *captivate* ✧ *portfolio* ✧ *argyle* ✧ *witness*
✧ *fertile* ✧ *eyebrow* ✧ *pentagram* ✧ *thirsty* ✧ *guidance*

Write the Story: **Stranded in a Foreign City**

Include the following in your story:

✧ *baptist* ✧ *assets* ✧ *cupcake* ✧ *showcase* ✧ *neurology*
✧ *workaday* ✧ *pine* ✧ *cushion* ✧ *assistant* ✧ *firmament*

Write the Story: **A Spy on the Job**

Include the following in your story:

✧ *apostle* ✧ *kitty* ✧ *myriad* ✧ *investment* ✧ *republic*
✧ *crimson* ✧ *flint* ✧ *postern* ✧ *original* ✧ *field*

Write the Story: **In The Middle of a Long, Cold Winter**

Include the following in your story:

✧ *opera* ✧ *redeem* ✧ *razor* ✧ *lungs* ✧ *grace*
✧ *futuristic* ✧ *tread* ✧ *vest* ✧ *milkshake* ✧ *powder*

Write the Story: **Something Valuable Has Been Stolen**

Include the following in your story:

✧ *huntress* ✧ *machinations* ✧ *trophy* ✧ *turncoat* ✧ *treasure*
✧ *minute* ✧ *nook* ✧ *historic* ✧ *rock* ✧ *ruin*

Write the Story: **A Famous Fictional Character in the Wrong Story**

Include the following in your story:

✧ *stock market* ✧ *serial* ✧ *tangy* ✧ *panda* ✧ *ensemble*
✧ *salute* ✧ *average* ✧ *Venus* ✧ *boss* ✧ *knee*

Write the Story: **A Talented Musician Struggles to Make It Big**

Include the following in your story:

✧ *crocodile* ✧ *anchor* ✧ *lasagna* ✧ *anthem* ✧ *fingernail*
✧ *trout* ✧ *federal* ✧ *bog* ✧ *jostle* ✧ *repel*

Write the Story: **A Family Gathering on a Holiday**

Include the following in your story:

✧ *rabbi* ✧ *irony* ✧ *bamboozle* ✧ *sturgeon* ✧ *bale*
✧ *reserve* ✧ *vanquish* ✧ *submerge* ✧ *plum* ✧ *rhetorical*

Write the Story: **The Main Character Ignored the Warning Label**

Include the following in your story:

✧ *comedian* ✧ *commission* ✧ *trump* ✧ *bamboo* ✧ *bombastic*
✧ *vast* ✧ *blonde* ✧ *gross* ✧ *sophisticated* ✧ *giraffe*

Write the Story: **Conversation on a Train**

Include the following in your story:

✧ *unicorn* ✧ *enslave* ✧ *steak* ✧ *maw* ✧ *plunge*
✧ *worthy* ✧ *recoil* ✧ *absolve* ✧ *suspenders* ✧ *worldwide*

Write the Story: **The Phone Rings at 3 A.M.**

Include the following in your story:

✧ *guerilla* ✧ *emerald* ✧ *careless* ✧ *traffic* ✧ *liberate*
✧ *adolescence* ✧ *punch* ✧ *wave* ✧ *environment* ✧ *oval*

Write the Story: **The Characters Are Aware That They're Fictional**

Include the following in your story:

✧ *oil rig* ✧ *dynasty* ✧ *lousy* ✧ *vault* ✧ *discharge*
✧ *supreme* ✧ *migrate* ✧ *harvest* ✧ *jaw* ✧ *pudding*

Write the Story: **Two People Who Hate Each Other Have to Cooperate**

Include the following in your story:

✧ *kidnap* ✧ *pinstripe* ✧ *quagmire* ✧ *lofty* ✧ *Adirondack*
✧ *pinky* ✧ *aftermath* ✧ *kernel* ✧ *legacy* ✧ *fail*

Write the Story: **The Story Begins at a Funeral**

Include the following in your story:

✧ *poker* ✧ *paramount* ✧ *earlobe* ✧ *marrow* ✧ *epic*
✧ *upgrade* ✧ *offshoot* ✧ *chihuahua* ✧ *episode* ✧ *icon*

Write the Story: **Five People from Completely Different Backgrounds Seated Together**

Include the following in your story:

✧ *Vietnam* ✧ *stakes* ✧ *sequel* ✧ *club* ✧ *lens*
✧ *draft* ✧ *perpetual* ✧ *otherwise* ✧ *groom* ✧ *hidden*

Write the Story: **Time Travel**

Include the following in your story:

✧ *hurricane* ✧ *email* ✧ *launder* ✧ *pastry* ✧ *garlic*
✧ *staff* ✧ *germs* ✧ *gallery* ✧ *brace* ✧ *share*

Write the Story: **Someone is Hiding in the Linen Closet**

Include the following in your story:

✧ *grandfather* ✧ *canoe* ✧ *pear* ✧ *cakewalk* ✧ *blouse*
✧ *assignment* ✧ *stampede* ✧ *present* ✧ *dinner* ✧ *slurp*

Write the Story: **A Deal with the Devil**

Include the following in your story:

✧ *regime* ✧ *album* ✧ *torch* ✧ *lodge* ✧ *highway*
✧ *sandy* ✧ *rune* ✧ *contract* ✧ *token* ✧ *suit*

Write the Story: **A Priest Hearing a Unique Confession**

Include the following in your story:

✧ *Chinese* ✧ *crustacean* ✧ *flash* ✧ *bucket* ✧ *vessel*
✧ *notice* ✧ *memoir* ✧ *brute* ✧ *docile* ✧ *cucumber*

Write the Story: **The Main Character is Startled Awake By ...**

Include the following in your story:

✧ *subway* ✧ *evergreen* ✧ *core* ✧ *emblem* ✧ *wild*
✧ *swine* ✧ *poised* ✧ *occupation* ✧ *inspector* ✧ *gate*

Write the Story: **Escaping a Natural Disaster**

Include the following in your story:

✧ *museum* ✧ *exonerate* ✧ *epicurean* ✧ *senseless* ✧ *literacy*
✧ *software* ✧ *solar* ✧ *tear* ✧ *coloring* ✧ *quarry*

Write the Story: **A Blind Date**

Include the following in your story:

✧ *park bench* ✧ *manager* ✧ *beastie* ✧ *honeydew* ✧ *justice*
✧ *manmade* ✧ *placement* ✧ *fabric* ✧ *prevention* ✧ *basket*

Write the Story: **A Hermit Is Forced to Go to a Crowded Place**

Include the following in your story:

- *typewriter*
- *water bottle*
- *lenient*
- *clerk*
- *render*
- *runner*
- *soil*
- *sewn*
- *chauffeur*
- *waterway*

Write the Story: **Caught in the Rain**

Include the following in your story:

✧ *Las Vegas* ✧ *radiology* ✧ *etch* ✧ *funeral* ✧ *textile*
✧ *sweep* ✧ *muslin* ✧ *wholesale* ✧ *wildlife* ✧ *English*

Write the Story: **A Couple Who Married Young**

Include the following in your story:

✧ *Monopoly* ✧ *flashlight* ✧ *aerospace* ✧ *exchange* ✧ *biology*
✧ *lawyer* ✧ *machinery* ✧ *revenge* ✧ *anthill* ✧ *concealed*

Write the Story: **A Myth That Explains a Common Natural Occurrence**

Include the following in your story:

✧ *river mouth* ✧ *punishment* ✧ *warehouse* ✧ *claim* ✧ *coder*
✧ *ache* ✧ *bend* ✧ *coop* ✧ *dam* ✧ *frown*

Write the Story: **A Nasty Rumor**

Include the following in your story:

✧ *Antarctica* ✧ *candy bar* ✧ *sympathetic* ✧ *minister* ✧ *patrol*
✧ *commonality* ✧ *auction* ✧ *bandage* ✧ *crush* ✧ *dive*

Write the Story: **A Lifelong Bachelor Visiting Married Friends**

Include the following in your story:

✧ *tick tock* ✧ *factory* ✧ *zoology* ✧ *arrest* ✧ *broadcast*
✧ *comb* ✧ *divorce* ✧ *flap* ✧ *harness* ✧ *gaze*

Write the Story: **A Mistake That Costs Someone's Life**

Include the following in your story:

✧ *Everglades* ✧ *bulletin* ✧ *fiend* ✧ *crew* ✧ *floss*
✧ *humor* ✧ *grease* ✧ *kiss* ✧ *link* ✧ *notice*

Write the Story: **A Good Reason to Be Afraid of the Dark**

Include the following in your story:

✧ *killer whale* ✧ *depraved* ✧ *janitor* ✧ *bargain* ✧ *dye*
✧ *fool* ✧ *heap* ✧ *kick* ✧ *praise* ✧ *quilt*

Write the Story: **Alone on a Deserted Island**

Include the following in your story:

✧ *book review* ✧ *organism* ✧ *mermaid* ✧ *bother* ✧ *decrease*
✧ *echo* ✧ *grimace* ✧ *inch* ✧ *march* ✧ *pump*

Write the Story: **A Fairy Tale in a Faraway Land**

Include the following in your story:

✧ *dragon* ✧ *strike* ✧ *collection* ✧ *guess* ✧ *joke*
✧ *smirk* ✧ *twist* ✧ *upstage* ✧ *wreck* ✧ *beaver*

Write the Story: **The Main Character Gets Rejected**

Include the following in your story:

✧ *office* ✧ *popcorn* ✧ *genial* ✧ *rhyme* ✧ *shampoo*
✧ *vote* ✧ *yawn* ✧ *baboon* ✧ *freak* ✧ *hag*

Write the Story: **A Divorced Couple is Stuck Together**

Include the following in your story:

✧ *twister* ✧ *specialist* ✧ *grate* ✧ *swivel* ✧ *elk*

✧ *arise* ✧ *assertive* ✧ *torment* ✧ *zest* ✧ *solvent*

Write the Story: **An Anniversary Party**

Include the following in your story:

✧ *tour guide* ✧ *sprout* ✧ *beluga* ✧ *breed* ✧ *galoshes*
✧ *bitterness* ✧ *adversary* ✧ *binary* ✧ *radiant* ✧ *transit*

Write the Story: **A Difficult Decision**

Include the following in your story:

✧ *Grand Canyon* ✧ *skate* ✧ *vacuum* ✧ *waltz* ✧ *grizzly*
✧ *cling* ✧ *brogue* ✧ *agony* ✧ *twinkling* ✧ *observatory*

Write the Story: **The Cast of a Broadway Show**

Include the following in your story:

✧ *gargoyle* ✧ *advertisement* ✧ *shelter* ✧ *cast* ✧ *calculating*
✧ *singularity* ✧ *dwarf* ✧ *arithmetic* ✧ *rubber* ✧ *scissors*

Write the Story: **A Summer Job**

Include the following in your story:

✧ *amusement park* ✧ *unrefined* ✧ *silence* ✧ *tease* ✧ *creep*
✧ *elated* ✧ *interstellar* ✧ *spiral* ✧ *quiz* ✧ *agent*

Write the Story: **Grandparents Acting Like Children**

Include the following in your story:

✧ *wedding* ✧ *squash* ✧ *dream* ✧ *foretell* ✧ *gluestick*
✧ *urchin* ✧ *solstice* ✧ *inertia* ✧ *ice* ✧ *composer*

Write the Story: **Keeping a Promise**

Include the following in your story:

✧ *abolitionist* ✧ *coyote* ✧ *forbid* ✧ *gloomy* ✧ *keen*
✧ *lesson* ✧ *genetics* ✧ *variable* ✧ *retort* ✧ *mass*

Write the Story: **Ten People in a Blackout**

Include the following in your story:

✧ *ballet* ✧ *thunder* ✧ *grind* ✧ *handwriting* ✧ *partner*
✧ *yardstick* ✧ *adopt* ✧ *swarm* ✧ *bundle* ✧ *prodigious*

Write the Story: **Shenanigans on a Movie Set**

Include the following in your story:

✧ *stunt* ✧ *wring* ✧ *lull* ✧ *stingy* ✧ *husband*
✧ *ginger* ✧ *buggy* ✧ *pedal* ✧ *llama* ✧ *anaconda*

Write the Story: **A Coup at a Secret Base**

Include the following in your story:

✧ *desert* ✧ *waylay* ✧ *pensive* ✧ *gazillions* ✧ *juniper*
✧ *helicopter* ✧ *lotus* ✧ *captain* ✧ *bandana* ✧ *taco*

Write the Story: **Halloween Night in a Hospital**

Include the following in your story:

✧ *centaur* ✧ *interweave* ✧ *placid* ✧ *benefactor* ✧ *peppermint*
✧ *gondola* ✧ *lambada* ✧ *twilight* ✧ *inlet* ✧ *throw*

Write the Story: **A Comedy of Errors**

Include the following in your story:

✧ *undead* ✧ *shrink* ✧ *quarrelsome* ✧ *harpy* ✧ *rickshaw*
✧ *limbo* ✧ *dusk* ✧ *cricket* ✧ *sunshine* ✧ *whoops*

Write the Story: **An Amateur Film Competition**

Include the following in your story:

✧ *asteroid* ✧ *multitude* ✧ *bobsled* ✧ *rodent* ✧ *boysenberry*
✧ *gut* ✧ *reel* ✧ *showtime* ✧ *buoy* ✧ *spider*

Write the Story: **An EMT Jinxes His/Herself by Hoping for a Quiet Shift**

Include the following in your story:

✧ *ambulance* ✧ *hamster* ✧ *schooner* ✧ *cane* ✧ *whiz*
✧ *outdoors* ✧ *euphoria* ✧ *cylindrical* ✧ *crisp* ✧ *painting*

Write the Story: **Last Call at a Bar in a Big City**

Include the following in your story:

✧ *doppelganger* ✧ *platypus* ✧ *jazz* ✧ *alienated* ✧ *bikini*
✧ *constitution* ✧ *batter* ✧ *temper* ✧ *basin* ✧ *rift*

Write the Story: **A Creature Feature in Present Day**

Include the following in your story:

✧ *werewolf* ✧ *barge* ✧ *caramel* ✧ *housefly* ✧ *awesome*
✧ *simmer* ✧ *analogy* ✧ *gulf* ✧ *femur* ✧ *amber*

Write the Story: **The Crew of a Commercial Fishing Boat**

Include the following in your story:

✧ *battleship* ✧ *whoosh* ✧ *colossal* ✧ *vertebrae* ✧ *salmon*
✧ *mahogany* ✧ *paddle* ✧ *breakfast* ✧ *gathering* ✧ *wheel*

Write the Story: **A Single Parent Solves a Problem**

Include the following in your story:

✧ *adoption* ✧ *grotesque* ✧ *cove* ✧ *snail* ✧ *olive*
✧ *navel* ✧ *rivulet* ✧ *hollow* ✧ *ambrosia* ✧ *pale*

Write the Story: **Blast from the Past**

Include the following in your story:

✧ *shrew* ✧ *happy-go-lucky* ✧ *esophagus* ✧ *handkerchief* ✧ *shred*
✧ *clause* ✧ *scone* ✧ *pewter* ✧ *biscuit* ✧ *necklace*

Write the Story: **A Dog Walker in Washington, DC**

Include the following in your story:

✧ *senator* ✧ *grotto* ✧ *strudel* ✧ *jade* ✧ *welcome*
✧ *slang* ✧ *complementary* ✧ *vacant* ✧ *jellyfish* ✧ *admonish*

Write the Story: **An Interview on Live TV**

Include the following in your story:

✧ *bishop* ✧ *impish* ✧ *amoeba* ✧ *sheep* ✧ *denim*
✧ *jet* ✧ *apricot* ✧ *sepia* ✧ *nipple* ✧ *bellow*

Write the Story: **It's a Setup!**

Include the following in your story:

✧ *acrobat* ✧ *blurt* ✧ *jolt* ✧ *gregarious* ✧ *tortoise*
✧ *persimmon* ✧ *balk* ✧ *follow* ✧ *gasp* ✧ *deli*

Write the Story: **Be Careful What You Wish For**

Include the following in your story:

✧ *toadstool* ✧ *bluff* ✧ *yodel* ✧ *thistle* ✧ *smock*
✧ *rust* ✧ *tomato* ✧ *bestow* ✧ *enunciate* ✧ *medium*

Write the Story: **A Hairbrained Scheme**

Include the following in your story:

✧ *entrepreneur* ✧ *vermilion* ✧ *hazmat* ✧ *bless* ✧ *cashier*
✧ *horseradish* ✧ *banjo* ✧ *melt* ✧ *modify* ✧ *woozy*

Write the Story: **Starting Over in a New Place**

Include the following in your story:

- *Dubai*
- *fedora*
- *sienna*
- *befriend*
- *grate*
- *listen*
- *heiress*
- *twinge*
- *mute*
- *charcoal*

Write the Story: **Tea Time in an English Inn**

Include the following in your story:

✧ *vampire* ✧ *tiara* ✧ *badlands* ✧ *brag* ✧ *empty*
✧ *mauve* ✧ *winged* ✧ *trillion* ✧ *axis* ✧ *cone*

Write the Story: **Right Under Their Noses**

Include the following in your story:

✧ *catamaran* ✧ *kaleidoscope* ✧ *barter* ✧ *sandcastle* ✧ *divide*
✧ *organ* ✧ *formula* ✧ *binocular* ✧ *lecture* ✧ *ivory*

Write the Story: **Cleaning the Attic Brings Back Memories**

Include the following in your story:

✧ *extravaganza* ✧ *watershed* ✧ *cajole* ✧ *zealous* ✧ *factor*
✧ *teal* ✧ *loosen* ✧ *whistle* ✧ *ogle* ✧ *lemonade*

Write the Story: **A Hostage Situation**

Include the following in your story:

✧ *Hawaiian* ✧ *growl* ✧ *kazoo* ✧ *pledge* ✧ *licorice*
✧ *karate* ✧ *lapel* ✧ *plug* ✧ *terracotta* ✧ *trickle*

Write the Story: **The New Chef's First Day on the Job**

Include the following in your story:

✧ *sultan* ✧ *pause* ✧ *scatter* ✧ *khaki* ✧ *sip*
✧ *undress* ✧ *waver* ✧ *marmalade* ✧ *snare* ✧ *ring*

Write the Story: **An Object Found in the Trash**

Include the following in your story:

✧ *cobbler* ✧ *umber* ✧ *haunt* ✧ *grumble* ✧ *raincoat*
✧ *unleavened* ✧ *bravery* ✧ *ray* ✧ *toffee* ✧ *imaginary*

Write the Story: **A New Life on a New Planet**

Include the following in your story:

✧ *negotiation* ✧ *churro* ✧ *postulate* ✧ *reiterate* ✧ *pullover*
✧ *contentment* ✧ *watermelon* ✧ *beech* ✧ *momentary* ✧ *frozen*

Write the Story: **An Encounter at Sea**

Include the following in your story:

✧ *commodore* ✧ *wisteria* ✧ *spoon* ✧ *indictment* ✧ *helix*
✧ *cavalry* ✧ *seal* ✧ *steeple* ✧ *fortnight* ✧ *smidgen*

Write the Story: **A New Customer Walks into the Shop**

Include the following in your story:

✧ *boudoir* ✧ *redwood* ✧ *west* ✧ *biography* ✧ *whiten*
✧ *sycophant* ✧ *mandatory* ✧ *commandment* ✧ *perform* ✧ *herbal*

Write the Story: **The Day Two Lifelong Friends Met**

Include the following in your story:

✧ *plantain* ✧ *greenhouse* ✧ *fleet* ✧ *premature* ✧ *lace*
✧ *possess* ✧ *divine* ✧ *culpable* ✧ *soulmate* ✧ *auspicious*

Write the Story: **A Team Comes Together**

Include the following in your story:

✧ *rugby* ✧ *mozzarella* ✧ *prism* ✧ *balsam* ✧ *channel*
✧ *puppet* ✧ *marvel* ✧ *quarrel* ✧ *contain* ✧ *parents*

Write the Story: **A Fan Fiction Writers' Group Meeting**

Include the following in your story:

✧ *hijack* ✧ *kiwi* ✧ *patience* ✧ *pendulum* ✧ *cunning*
✧ *leaden* ✧ *resign* ✧ *dawn* ✧ *fury* ✧ *mock*

Write the Story: **A Cabaret Singer's Night Off**

Include the following in your story:

✧ *kimono* ✧ *profound* ✧ *hypnotize* ✧ *caprice* ✧ *mutter*
✧ *custom* ✧ *oppress* ✧ *local* ✧ *cash* ✧ *unwittingly*

Write the Story: **Revisiting a Fond Memory**

Include the following in your story:

✧ *grief* ✧ *evidence* ✧ *covenant* ✧ *churn* ✧ *piazza*
✧ *intention* ✧ *vanish* ✧ *honeymoon* ✧ *careful* ✧ *crowd*

Write the Story: **A Second Chance**

Include the following in your story:

✧ *probation* ✧ *turbine* ✧ *pentagon* ✧ *renew* ✧ *flirt*
✧ *mindful* ✧ *dragonfly* ✧ *lukewarm* ✧ *hoot* ✧ *club*

Write the Story: **Scientists Are Never Off Duty**

Include the following in your story:

✧ *fossil* ✧ *reactor* ✧ *sage* ✧ *hell* ✧ *gluten*
✧ *devour* ✧ *fig* ✧ *landmine* ✧ *babble* ✧ *New Year*

Write the Story: **Nerds in a Heated Argument**

Include the following in your story:

✧ *tesseract* ✧ *synthesis* ✧ *padawan* ✧ *icebreaker* ✧ *chomp*
✧ *decipher* ✧ *utility* ✧ *keepsake* ✧ *slush* ✧ *croak*

Write the Story: **The Closing Arguments of a Big Case**

Include the following in your story:

✧ *courtroom* ✧ *wheelhouse* ✧ *catapult* ✧ *emit* ✧ *clamp*
✧ *peanut* ✧ *ticket* ✧ *vapor* ✧ *thimble* ✧ *decree*

Write the Story: **Retired Veterans Telling Their War Stories**

Include the following in your story:

✧ *internment* ✧ *fret* ✧ *kneel* ✧ *fasten* ✧ *drizzle*
✧ *nursery* ✧ *abundantly* ✧ *scarce* ✧ *discourteous* ✧ *grant*

Write the Story: **Old Friends Meet Over Coffee**

Include the following in your story:

✧ *Algonquin* ✧ *amazement* ✧ *elm* ✧ *tobacco* ✧ *hiss*
✧ *digress* ✧ *echo* ✧ *immense* ✧ *quiet* ✧ *opaque*

Write the Story: **Follow the Main Character Through a Day with No Dialog or Direct Interactions**

Include the following in your story:

✧ *sociopath* ✧ *buzz* ✧ *mend* ✧ *geyser* ✧ *awl*
✧ *consent* ✧ *diner* ✧ *second-hand* ✧ *vice* ✧ *wane*

Write the Story: **A Wedding Reception with Hundreds of Guests**

Include the following in your story:

✧ *war* ✧ *nag* ✧ *omit* ✧ *Ramadan* ✧ *downpour*

✧ *vouch* ✧ *loop* ✧ *gridlock* ✧ *allegro* ✧ *Filipino*

Write the Story: **The Hottest Day of the Year**

Include the following in your story:

✧ *suspense* ✧ *dogwood* ✧ *speculate* ✧ *playground* ✧ *peel*
✧ *avenue* ✧ *moderation* ✧ *classical* ✧ *yummy* ✧ *bluster*